Breathe In, Breathe Out

How I Overcame Sensorimotor OCD

Alexander Culafi

Contents

Part I

Introduction

I just want to start this off by saying, hey, I get it. I know how bad sensorimotor OCD is, how bad it makes you feel, the hopelessness that comes from it, how little people understand you, and how you feel like you will never escape the hell that is being hyper aware of something, be it your own breath, your blinking, swallowing, sound, movement, specific body parts on other people's bodies, floaters, ear ringing, and other physical awarenesses I might not have even mentioned. I get it.

My battle against hyperawareness/sensorimotor OCD began on a Saturday in July, 2018, when I noticed that I noticed my breathing. I panicked, dreamt about it that night, and so began a hell that was noticing my breath (something you do notice but not that often) hundreds of times a day. In, out, in, out, in, out. I was troubled by the sensation, I was troubled by the sound, and I was worried that once I noticed it, I was never going to unnoticed it again. That started a loop of fear in my head that continued on and on for months. It's the thing that turned my bad OCD into crippling OCD, and the thing that started my spiral downwards (a spiral I eventually recovered from, spoiler alert!). After that, it became a hyperawareness of blinking, then of movement, then of other assorted things, but it was all the same silly pattern: *What if I never stop noticing this thing?*

My war with OCD was an intense one. The war involved a 9-day stay at a psychiatric hospital, a lot of suffering, a lot of imposition and stress on my loved ones, months and months of medication management, and the greatest challenges my life has had to date. That said, for now and hopefully ever (though I won't take such things for granted), I believe I'm on the other side of the worst of it. I don't know if I'm fully recovered (can one ever be?) but I sure am recovering well, and I sure am proud of it.

This is going to be a short book because I want to get straight to the point, or at least as fast to the point as possible. You need help, you need help now, and while I am no medical doctor or therapist (READ: I AM NOT A DOCTOR OR THERAPIST, SO DON'T TREAT THIS AS GOSPEL. IF YOU HAVE THE MEANS TO GET PROFESSIONAL HELP, PLEASE DO SO), I sure am an experienced patient of this not-often-enough discussed form of OCD. Stuff has very clearly worked for me. Some of those things are insights, and some of them are actual strategies. I will be sharing both with you..

While you're here, here are a few words of hope. Sensorimotor OCD is not a death sentence. You can escape this hell. It is possible, and not too hard to do with a little bit of time and elbow grease. I'm on the other side of this thing, and I believe you can be too.

This is the book I wish I had when I was going through this for the first time. I hope you enjoy it, and thank you for reading.

Part II

My Story

Note: Parts of this section and others were originally written as a blog post for TheOCDStories.com, home to a wonderful blog and podcast that I recommend as a resource to everyone with OCD.

It was a Wednesday night like any other. June 27, 2018. I had finished work for the day in my Brookline, MA apartment, went to the gym, came home, and got ready to make dinner. My girlfriend had gone vegan a couple months before and, while I was still eating animal products, I started integrating more non-meat foods into my diet. Tonight, I was trying a new sunflower-based veggie burger.

The veggie burger was microwavable, so I put it in for a couple minutes, got a potato bun ready, and went to plate it alongside carrot sticks and hummus. I then sat in front of my computer, watching a Joe Rogan clip about the new *God of War* game.

I took a bite of my veggie burger, and out of nowhere, my throat got immediately sore.

I have a pollen allergy that causes a similar effect when I eat some fresh fruit and it's generally harmless, so I kept eating thinking it would go away. It did not. I finished the veggie burger, and it got worse. I started to panic, so I looked around my room for Benadryl. When there was none, I decided to run to the supermarket, which was still open for another 30 minutes and was a short distance away. I ran there, looked around, and started sneezing uncontrollably. I bought children's Benadryl since it was the first one I saw, bought some Claritin, and noticed my face felt weird. When I got home, I took the medicine and Googled anaphylaxis to see how my story lined up with it. I was like, eh, a couple things line up, but I wasn't quite sure.

I figured it might be time to go to the ER, so I walked to the freezer and took a picture of the veggie burger. I walked past the kitchen mirror and noticed that my eyes had gotten puffy and blue, so I naturally said, *"Oh shit, time to go to the hospital."*

My closest ER is a 15-minute walk away, so I thought instead of waiting for an ambulance (I could still breathe through my mouth), I would run to the hospital. An EpiPen is adrenaline, so I figured running would be a smart thing to do, right? Dumb mistake. Exercise makes it worse. If you ever have to go through this, and I pray you don't, call 9-1-1. If you ever wonder whether you should call 9-1-1, that's the precise time to call 9-1-1. It didn't get remarkably worse, but when I got to the ER they didn't even let me sit down. They made me sign a paper and then a nurse walked me straight back into treatment, where she felt for a vein, hooked up an IV, and put Benadryl into my veins immediately.

When they put a warm cloth over my eyes, I asked myself, "Am I dying right now?" and as my life flashed before me, I started panicking because at age 23 (at the time), I was, surprisingly, not ready to go. They reassured me I wasn't going to die, told me I was having an acute allergic reaction, and that even if I didn't go to the ER, I might have had difficulty breathing but that's it. That said, to have a fear of death build up over the course of your life and then to simply taste life's uncertainty for the first time while watching The Joe Rogan Experience? Now that's scary. I'd say traumatizing.

They kept an eye on me until about 3 a.m. (four hours is the standard for these events, but sometimes it's overnight if the reaction is bad enough). They wrote me a prescription for Benadryl, prednisone, and an EpiPen pack, and I got to bed at 4.

The next morning, I was in a bit of a daze.

What happened? What was I allergic to? Was it the veggie burger? If so, which ingredients? Or was it something else? No, it definitely had to be the veggie burger. Well, the only allergic ingredients it could have been were sunflower seeds and carrots. Was it sunflower seed? Maybe it was sunflower seed.

I got myself a tuna melt from the nearby diner and began to question every food choice I'd made in adulthood. What activated in me? Do I have peanut allergies? I have peanut butter nearly every day but I know a kid who almost died from that allergy so maybe me too?

When I picked up the EpiPen prescription they wrote me at the hospital, I felt like I had come face-to-face with a now-constant reminder of my fragility and mortality. I tested the included practice EpiPen on myself many, many times. But who knows if it would save me, right? I saw an allergy doctor who explained to me that I was fine if I stuck to foods I recognized but needed to get my blood and skin tested to make sure everything was safe. I got the blood tested and set up a skin test for the following week.

For the rest of that week and weekend, I was in a strange, distrustful, anxious, ruminating state. Nothing was explicitly wrong with me and I hadn't had any real heavy panic attacks, but I was in a constant state of vigilance and distrust for every piece of food I came into contact with.

Sunday was good, initially.

Once a month, I get together with two of my best friends, Matt and Mason, and we record a podcast about all manner of fun topics. Frozen pizzas, video game ideas, pet peeves, and other such things. We all go to the same apartment in Arlington, MA and record a handful of episodes to go up on our Soundcloud, after which point we get pizza, shoot the hay, and call it a day. That night, we went to the pizza place and I got a tuna sub--my signature--and then we went to an ice cream parlor connected to a movie theater to get a nice dessert. I got an ice cream cookie with a cookies-and-cream filling in the middle.

I'm not sure what it was, but something in that moment snapped. I was eating the ice cream cookie, and I felt like I was going to have an allergic reaction. My throat dried up, my eyes got wide, I got extremely paranoid and antsy, and I went to the bathroom to calm myself down. I waited all hands on deck in the empty movie theater bathroom for nothing to happen, looked in the mirror for changes while I began to feel nauseated, went back to my friends, and paced back and forth in front of them before catching myself and sitting down. They didn't notice anything was wrong, surprisingly, but I didn't feel good and decided not to continue eating the ice cream sandwich.

On the Uber ride home, my nausea increased and increased.

I got back home to my girlfriend who, by that point, was ready to go to sleep. She had been spending a few days with me while I got over this paranoid state of mine--little did either of us realize how much this would impact my life for the foreseeable future.

That night, I couldn't sleep, and I spent the entire night hunched over a toilet for a vomit that never came. I went to the ER the following night because I felt an intense pain like my chest and stomach was on fire. Thinking I had GERD, they gave me omeprazole, sucralfate, and told me to see my primary care doctor.

The following month involved me taking stomach drugs for intense nausea and heartburn while getting scared every time I ate something, thinking it was going to kill me via allergic reaction. I had panic attack after panic attack, and in addition, I was afraid that I was either going to die or throw up in my sleep—or both. I still have no idea how that fear developed. I also developed an intense hypochondria during this time period. One day I thought I had appendicitis. The next, stomach cancer. The day after that, colon cancer. I told myself that each subsequent disease was going to be the one that got me. My sleep fell to roughly five hours a night.

I realized, thankfully, that my mental health was in an unsustainable state, and my solution was to try everything I could. I began meditating both on my own and with Headspace (a guided meditation app), I took on a serious exercise regiment, I studied CBT with *When Panic Attacks* by David Burns, and I read books by people like Claire Weekes. I buried myself in work, went on visits to see family members, used tried-and-true coping mechanisms—the works. I tried it all, and the more I tried, the worse it got.

I found out after a month or so via endoscopy that I didn't have any stomach issues, and that said issues were likely a combination of anxiety and the drugs I was taking.

And so, my stomach felt better, but my anxiety marched on. In addition to random panic attacks and a fear of sleep, I started to get weirder issues, like songs stuck in my head for days at a time alongside a fear that I would never let go of them. This may have been my first sign of OCD. Before any of this happened, the only OCD-like trait I really had was that I checked the stove a handful of times before bed every night, but I lived with four other roommates so doing so didn't feel unreasonable.

Everything continued until one Saturday sometime in July, when I wondered if I was going to forget to breathe. As a result, I began to get obsessed with my own breathing. In, out, in out, hundreds of times a day. It drove me absolutely nuts over the following weeks, and I thought I was never going to lose awareness over my breathing.

I went to Google and discovered something called "sensorimotor OCD" in some places, with some people posting that they were dealing with it for years, that it was horrible, that they couldn't escape it, and that, in some cases, they were having dark, hopeless thoughts to the extent of suicidal ideation. I was convinced that this breathing obsession was something I was going to have to deal with for the rest of my life. That it was going to be the death of me.

My solution was to practice meditation until I perfected my practice and the scary thoughts and sensations would no longer hold power over me. It was my last hope to beat these demons.

Only, as I tried to meditate and practice more coping mechanisms, everything, once again, kept getting worse. My breathing obsession improved and I built up a tolerance, but it was replaced by obsessions with the blinking of myself and others, followed by weird intrusive thoughts and images, followed by an obsession with the feeling of the inside of my mouth, followed by an obsession with the feeling of air on my skin, followed by an obsession with movement, followed by obsessions with the colors red and white for no clear reason. I was scared I would never let go of these awarenesses, and that I would be trapped in this state forever and ever.

The one that broke the camel's back was one in early September where I questioned whether anything outside my peripheral vision was real, and I questioned whether things existed or were just hallucinations. Google, my trusty "friend," suggested I could have a delusion disorder, which is, so I read, one of the worst things in the mental health world. I didn't actually believe my thoughts, mind you, but my mind kept coming up with intrusive thoughts questioning it all, and I listened. I would later learn that existential crises were totally common in the OCD world, but I didn't know that at the time, so I went back to the ER for a mental health evaluation.

After a day of waiting in the emergency room, they thought I had a mood disorder like bipolar, and suggested that I go inpatient. I made the decision because I knew I needed medicine and ran out of patience to see a psychiatrist long enough to get the right med balance. So I went from having no psychiatric experience (nor need for it) to, three months later, spending nine days at a psychiatric hospital.

At the hospital, the nurse practitioner there thought that the prednisone I had been given for my allergic reaction made me crazy, which it had been known to do to some people. Not bipolar. They gave me Zyprexa and Luvox, and let me go ultimately because I wasn't actually suicidal and didn't really belong there even though I didn't feel better by any means.

After being discharged, I went to a partial hospitalization program where I went to five groups a day and met with a counselor once a week for about a month or so. Contrary to the initial bipolar and prednisone-based diagnoses, she said she thought I had OCD (which is what I originally thought I had before the obsessions got scarier). She also introduced me to *The Happiness Trap* by Russ Harris (an amazing, amazing book) as well as some initial ACT concepts.

But because the Luvox hadn't fully kicked in yet and because I didn't fully grasp the ACT skills, my obsessions continued to get worse in the PHP, and I thought I'd have to go back to the hospital. I even, at one point, developed a proper harm obsession (I was afraid that, almost like a werewolf, I would lose control, sleepwalk in my sleep, and harm myself despite having no desire nor history of such things). It was not good. I also found a psychiatrist at this time who I told my story to, and he said, I quote, that I was "f*cked" (thankfully I did not see him a second time, and my next prescriber neither said nor believed such things as far as I know).

And then, two things happened. The first is that, despite my life being a nightmare of obsessions and questioning reality, the Luvox started to kick in, and I began to slowly-but-surely retake control of my life. The second is that, on the official International OCD Foundation website, I tracked down a therapist that specializes in OCD treatment. I found a brilliant dude named Gabe who taught me all about how OCD works and how to properly utilize ACT skills. He explained that I had a rare OCD called hyperawareness OCD (referred to in this book mostly as sensorimotor OCD) and that it was treatable through exposure work and ACT. I began learning to drop the struggle and let my mind do what it's going to do, all while living my life in the process.

After this, in early 2019, I went on The OCD Stories podcast, a podcast and blog (I participated in content for both) that features professionals in the field of OCD as well as those with the condition, and I recommend the podcast to anyone who wants to learn more about OCD without going down the compulsion rabbit hole of

Googling themselves into oblivion. On the blog post I wrote for The OCD Stories (I used a good deal of it in this book, with permission), I included my Twitter handle and told people to reach out if they have more questions. Since then, I've received Facebook and Twitter messages from 2-3 dozen people looking for help with sensorimotor OCD. Some people I helped, some people I provided what resources I could, and I did my best to give everyone who contacted me a safe next step in continuing their journey of OCD recovery. Regardless, these experiences made me want to put all of what I learned over the past two years into a book that can be used to help others with this curious yet (I believe) not-that-uncommon form of OCD.

Other than that, my last year and change has been spent conducting medication management with a wonderful prescriber named Rosilyn who helped me find a great med balance with small-to-no side effects, and improving constantly with only minor hiccups here and there. Today, I would call myself recovering, if not recovered. My sensorimotor OCD is kept in check with the following strategies you're about to see, and medication has been treating me well. I still think about my breathing over the course of the day, but much less than I used to, and I think that over time, I could go back to normal levels of thinking about my breathing/blinking/swallowing. I'm very close, and I think with these tools, you too can get further than you have before in treating your sensorimotor OCD. If nothing else, I want this book to give you hope that you can get to a much better place than you are right now. I believe in you.

Part III

How I Overcame Sensorimotor OCD

What you're about to read is my easy-to-apply, multi-pronged technique for dealing with breathing obsessions, but it can be applied to any hyperawareness obsession, and I've applied it to other types of obsessions I have. While I will make no guarantees, I believe that if a person suffering from sensorimotor OCD follows these steps, they can, at the very least, double his or her tolerance to it and start the journey towards effectively defeating this troubling, not-talked-about-enough disorder.

Step 1: Let it Be

If your mind wants to be aware of its breathing, or blinking, or swallowing, let it be. As long as it wants. As long as it takes.

If you're scared of being aware of your breathing, and this makes you aware of your breathing, the best thing to do...is nothing. Accept your situation, and let yourself be aware of these bodily sensations. Don't hold your breath, don't prevent yourself from blinking, and don't prevent yourself from swallowing your saliva. Just let yourself have those awarenesses: breathe, blink, swallow as much as you need to. Your body knows how to regulate itself. You won't forget to breathe or blink even though as I write that you're now doubting yourself.

If you're like me, you might find that the less resistance you put up and the longer you sit with these feelings and are open to them, your mind will start to get bored of being scared of your sensorimotor function(s), and the anxiety will slowly but surely recede into the back of your head until, day by day, it bothers you less and less. More importantly, you'll be aware of your sensorimotor function(s) less and less. And when those hyper-awarenesses come back, as they will, do it again. And again. And again. Over time, the process will likely become more automatic and you will just sit with your breathing sensation while barely noticing it.

That's the big secret of this book in a few paragraphs. Let it be, give it time, keep with it, and you will probably get better. Don't panic. Don't Google. Don't try various "tricks" (compulsions) to ease your anxiety. Just let it be. There's no trick to that. It's just about giving up the fight and sitting with your anxiety.

Quickly, you might realize that this worst thing ever is actually not that bad. You can be aware of your breathing and enjoy the company of your family at the same time. Or watch TV. Or enjoy dinner. And when you look at it that way, you actually realize being aware of your breathing is like a 3/10 annoyance and not a 9/10. And the annoyance might even go down from there.

Step 2: Do Your Best

Just do your best, especially if you get caught in the "is it a compulsion" trap. What do I mean by that? Well, as you start doing exposures for OCD, you might wonder if you're secretly doing compulsions because OCD bathes in uncertainty. Any time you're struggling, anytime you're unsure, just know that you're doing your best. Whatever happens happens. But also, there's no way to know for sure if you're doing a compulsion, and you just have to live with it. All you can do is your best.

Step 3: Know That the Mind is Always Changing, AKA Let Time Pass

Once I realized this, everything clicked and became a lot less scary. Ready? Here goes. Nothing is forever, *and that's a good thing*. The mind is always changing and never stays in one place. You physically cannot be fixated on something permanently, forever. When you go "oh no, I had a thought! Now I'll never stop having that thought!" or "oh no, I'll be fixated on this thing forever!" Don't worry. You'll move on from it, even if only for a little while. No matter how extreme the thought is, it's just a thought, and you will move on from it even if it comes back. If a song is looping in your head, it will go away. If you're fixated on breathing, it will pass even if (when) it comes back. But it'll always pass. It's never forever. As such, letting time pass is borderline magical. Anything that's on your mind, something else will be on your mind soon enough afterward and the thing you were worried about being there forever will, even if temporarily, be clean and gone. Knowing that gave me a lot of power.

As an aside, if you meditate, you might eventually start to notice what the present moment feels like. In the present moment, fully invested, your hyperawarenesses will almost certainly cease to be. Or they won't. You get it. Live with the uncertainty. But also, the present moment is your first weapon against OCD, and that present moment brain muscle is one worth training.

Remember: Thoughts are just thoughts. Even the scariest ones. Even the existential ones. Even the ones where you think you're aware of thought itself. Thoughts are just thoughts.

Step 4: Consume Good Resources

Not just what you read on Google! I've read a lot of books about OCD and a lot of books that helped me overcome my OCD. Here are three that I think everyone with OCD should read.

The Happiness Trap: How to Stop Struggling and Start Living: A Guide to ACT by Dr. Russ Harris

ACT is an incredible form of therapy that, outside of medicine, became my primary way of dealing with my intrusive thoughts and obsessions. The therapy is a combination of acceptance strategies and mindfulness that asks one to, rather than struggle with thoughts and fight them, do nothing and let your mind do what it's going to do. And, when you drop the struggle and move your efforts towards taking valued actions, you can create a life of meaning (and the thought-demons you're struggling with hold far less power over you). The Happiness Trap is a wonderful book that goes over these principles in detail, and I highly, highly, highly recommend anyone with OCD to give it a shot. It's been crucial to my recovery.

In addition to ACT, I recommend looking into the cognitive distortions piece of CBT, which tackles the irrational, unhelpful thought patterns we often find ourselves in. Learning about some of the more common pitfalls has been very helpful.

The Mindfulness Workbook for OCD: A Guide to Overcoming Obsessions and Compulsions Using Mindfulness and Cognitive Behavioral Therapy by Jon Hershfield and Tom Corboy

This OCD workbook is great and offers a mindfulness-based approach, but I like it because it actually has a chapter on hyperawareness OCD.

Getting Over OCD, Second Edition: A 10-Step Workbook for Taking Back Your Life by Dr. Jonathan Abramowitz

An overall great book for understanding and treating OCD.

In addition to the above books, I recommend checking out The OCD Stories, a podcast and blog that features OCD experts as well as those with the condition discussing OCD with a wonderful host named Stuart Ralph. Seriously, pick an episode you're interested in and listen to it at least once. You (probably, who knows?) won't regret it.

Oh yeah, and check out Dr. Claire Weekes. She's the one who figured out anxiety before anyone else did.

Step 5: If You Need Help, Ask for It

You are worth it. The world needs you. You are valuable and deserve to recover.

Enough said

Part IV

Other Things That May Help

Here's a section for recommendations that may or may not be helpful to you.

Read Stoicism

Stoicism is a school of philosophy that, among other things, teaches that we should accept the moment that presents itself and find meaning in what life has dealt us—to use our challenges in life to become greater human beings. Learning about philosophy might sound a little bit silly here, but it allowed me to find meaning in my suffering. It allowed me to say that if I can get through this, I can help other people get through it too someday. I recommend *The Obstacle is The Way* by Ryan Holiday and *Meditations* by Marcus Aurelius (Gregory Hays translation).

Exercise

Straightforward enough! Training your body has a few key benefits. In addition to making you look better and feel better, exercise provides an outlet to get some of that pent-up energy out of your system. It also gives you something to work towards in a time when you really need to work towards something.

Meditate

For me, meditation allows me to train my concentration and build up a greater tolerance for distress. If you want to get started, I recommend both *10% Happier* books by Dan Harris. One is more of an autobiography, and the other is a guide for various meditations to try. You can also look into Headspace if you want to try guided meditation (which is easier). My one piece of advice is to not expect too much out of meditation once it starts to help you. It'll take about a week or two to get any kind of benefit, and while the benefits are great over time, it won't fix your problems. Learning how to grapple with your thoughts through exposure work and ACT will provide more immediate benefit, I believe. That said, meditation has proved to be an excellent tool in the tool kit for me.

Look into an OCD Therapist

I didn't think it would be such a game-changer for me, but it was. Look up OCD therapists and find one well-reviewed that you trust. For me, my therapists (hi Kate and Gabe!) were invaluable in teaching me the principles of ACT and proper exposure (ERP) work. If you have OCD, exposure work is going to likely be a necessity in feeling better (yep, even for less-common ones like the sensorimotor/hyperawareness OCD I have), and working with a professional can make things go a lot smoother than trying to use Google as your OCD coach. I recommend the IOCDF website as a first resource.

Please Don't Google

It will hurt you, in the end, every single time you Google symptoms unnecessarily—especially if you have hypochondria. See a doctor if you need to, but Google will, in all likelihood, make you think you have something you actually don't.

It's Okay to Take Medication

I come from the school of thought that you should take as little medication as necessary, but there are good medications out there that can change the way you think for the better and healthier. Medication has been a game-changer for me. It allowed me to get sleep and get some peace and quiet in my mind I didn't have before. That said, only take medication prescribed to you by a prescriber, and when you get a prescriber (if you decide that's a path you want to go down), find a good, compassionate one. Remember it can take time, however, to get one you click with. It took me a couple tries to find one that worked for me.

A little aside: Before I went into the hospital and started taking medicine, my depression had gotten so severe that I wasn't eating or sleeping much at all. I didn't have the ability to properly tackle my OCD until I took care of the depression side of things, which medicine most certainly helped with. If your OCD has gotten to the point where you're severely depressed, you might need to handle the depression before tackling the OCD is even possible. Medicine helped me and others in this department. Just food for thought.

Part V

Conclusion

If you got this far, I just want to say thank you for listening, and I hope this helps. This OCD thing came close to ruining my life (or at least felt like it), and it was hard work, dedication, persistence, and the help of many others who got me here. I want to thank a few of them specifically.

Thank you Bailey, for being the best partner I could ever ask for.

Thank you Lena and Rula, for being there and listening even at the very worst moments. I don't think I could have done this without you.

Thank you Mom, for introducing me to Claire Weekes, and thank you and Dad for everything else you do (which is a lot!).

Thank you, Keith, for being an amazingly understanding boss during my time of need, as well as a great friend.

Thank you, Nouno, for encouraging me to put this book out.

And thank you for reading!

If you have any other questions, feel free to reach out via my website, www.alexculafi.com.